JAPANESE COLORING BOOK
FOR ADULTS

by Heather McLaughlin

Published by Performance Marketing Group, Inc.
8584 Washington Suite 2043
Chagrin Falls, Ohio 44034

www.heathermmclaughlin.com

For permssion contact: gifts@heathermmclaughlin.com

JAPAN

書畫新聞紙東京

JAPAN

「今日は日本」
日本とその文化。

日本
JAPAN
Japan

愛